A Horse Called Victory

A Horse Called Victory

Poems by

Timothy Tarkelly

© 2023 Timothy Tarkelly. All rights reserved.
This material may not be reproduced in any form, published,
reprinted, recorded, performed, broadcast,
rewritten or redistributed without
the explicit permission of Timothy Tarkelly.
All such actions are strictly prohibited by law.

Cover photo by Jeanne Hatch
Cover design by Shay Culligan
Author photo by Kevin Rabas

ISBN: 978-1-63980-461-0

Kelsay Books
502 South 1040 East, A-119
American Fork, Utah 84003
Kelsaybooks.com

For TJ and Adam, two sons of the somewhat West.

Acknowledgments

Thank you to the following publications, where versions of these poems previously appeared:

Agape Review: "San Miguel Chapel"

Ekstasis Magazine: "Saint Francis Ministers to the Owls at Rogue River"

The Grindstone: "Prairie Thoughts #5"

Plant People, an Anthology of Environmental Artists: "Cacti"

Rusty Truck: "Jesse James Was a Coward"

Contents

A Horse Called Victory	15
Last Stand at the Alamo	16
Thoreau Resists the Mexican War	17
Prairie Thoughts #1	19
Sin Twister	20
Jesse James Was a Coward	21
Friends	22
Cortina Strikes Down the Old Order	23
Texas Rangers	24
Mustang	25
Free Soil Party	26
Tecumseh to the Osages	27
The Railroad Is Coming	28
Clark's Hill	29
The Boys Come Home	30
The Abandoned Camp	31
Blood Money	33
Beecher's Bibles	34
All the Feathers I Sent Home	35
Prairie Thoughts #2	36
Heaven Is a Woman from Tennessee	37
Six Paces	38
Custer at Gettysburg	39
Ownership	40
Crockett for Congress	41
A Horse Called Dandy	42
Welcome to Yankton	43
Law Rules the Desert Shore	44
Prairie Thoughts #3	45
The Advice of Secretary Delano	46
Steer	47
Murieta	48
Cacti	49

Welcome to Kansas	50
Grant Is a Drinkin' Man	51
Custer Never Touches Liquor	52
San Isidro Smiles Over the Western Plains	53
Prairie Thoughts #4	54
Earp	55
Crazy Horse Scares Us Senseless	56
Marion	57
Tecumseh to Harrison	58
Locoweed	59
Georgetown	60
Dry Gulch Saloon	61
Cattleman's Lullaby	62
Pirate Savior of New Orleans	63
David Crockett to Charles Schultz	64
San Miguel Chapel	65
Annie Oakley	66
Prairie Thoughts #5	67
Red River Gonna Swallow You Whole	68
Chief Seattle's Alleged Oration	69
Pony Express	70
Weatherford	71
Westinghouse	72
Migrants Build the West	73
Saint Francis Ministers to the Owls at Rogue River	74
Fort Union	75
Custer Dies at Little Bighorn	76
Prairie Thoughts #6	77

*The dark chapters of American history
have just as much to teach us, if not more,
than the glorious ones, and often the two are intertwined.*
—Ken Burns

Make me as I am . . .
—Andrew Jackson to his sculptor

A Horse Called Victory

> "A horse disappoints those who trust in it for victory;
> despite its great strength it cannot deliver."
> —Psalm 33:17 (NET)

You can't fake it.
It takes a real leader to mold horseflesh,

a clean resection of instinct
with nothing but a soothing voice and a curry comb

to suit its heart and hide
for the hunt.

Mean hooves headlong toward hurt
and a yucca-browed madness

scraping the Earth clean
of its last civil notions.

Chestnut and leather
flared with white sparks.

Iron knuckled, steaming.
Ready for a reckoning.

How much heat does it take
to cook your biggest fears into engine coal?

It's all war dust.
Black powder nimbus,

a heavenscape
painted in broad strokes of lead

broken by earth and muscle,
spurs shattering against the skin.

Last Stand at the Alamo

The church bells rang under a hail of musket balls. Knives fell from the sky and landed in the right palms.

Could you hear Saint Michael? He dared us to carve "freedom" in Satan's forearm. Invite him in and see who could hold on the longest.

Thoreau Resists the Mexican War

Militant tempers choose sides too quickly.

Bring chaos and polished rifles

to the border of Eden,

open fire.

They try stitching landscapes together,

confiscate thread from the looms

of innocent women.

Aim at the cliffs, set camp

between any four mountains they choose.

Greedy eyes glued to all apertures,

shooting at will.

They'll stay there

until they've run out of ammo

and have launched each stone into service.

But hungry soldiers can't march.

No beans, no bacon.

Cut them off at the stomach.

Send the butchers home,

reroute supply lines,

feed the starving children

in our streets.

Wars cost money and a clean conscience

can't be bought. It's appraised

at the final judgment. Holy words

and posterity's memory for ulterior gain.

We civilized few

turn our backs on conquest,

worldly pursuits of fame.

I'll render unto Caesar what he has coming.

But as for all I have, I've earned it.

It's mine.

Prairie Thoughts #1

God makes bugs out of searing embers
and men out of weak leather.
Can't sleep in camp.
Thorn scars and sweat rash
violently kiss me to sleep.
Pricks of blood in the morning,
black filth for coffee.
Always pissing into the wind.

Sin Twister

Knee deep in a one-mule stream.
Mud and shining rock.

Calling all lost children who wander,
grow tired of counting the clouds
in a clear sky, who can finally see the sun
for its fire.

A hoarse cadence beckons
a generous flood,
promises a lay-in-wait,
a temporary grave and loose dirt.

A day that will shred the sod
as good folks rise,
war horns bleeding the blue heavens,
washing every inch of us clean.

Jesse James Was a Coward

Jesse James was a coward,
a half-cocked trigger
pulled from a Kansas City paper
where rich folks long since cornered
the market on low rent heroes,
sore loser complexes
as deep as the Missouri, as wide as Missouri,
as miserable as the gray-coated, blood stained
losers who came back to sharecrop their way
through life, drink their Kentucky hang-ups,
leave the local swill for the federals.
He carved Dixie on his lips and bit every time
he heard someone whistle the Star-Spangled Banner.
Train robbing, shooting bankers just for looking like
America. A place he lived, cursed for welcoming him back home,
whose ground he filled with shallow graves and
thin definitions of liberty. One of those
feeble-minded outlaws
who never could realize they're not special.
They, too, must give thanks for what they have
rather than burn us for what they don't.

Friends

The light comes in,
windows and doorways,
shoulders that lift, make room
for simple breaths,
prayerful motion, and stolid calm.
We sit amidst the stillness,
thank God for pure water,
a cleanliness that peels at the surface,
bathes the wayfaring spirit,
carries new gifts
to wherever the meek
are willing to receive them.

Cortina Strikes Down the Old Order

You can pull both respect and fear
from either end of a pistol.
Blast clean through notions
of princely form.
Let actions speak for themselves.
A new form of rule,
a whole chunk of country
governed by legend,
morality that flints beneath the feet,
has the townsfolk crossing themselves
whenever the name is mentioned.
Of course, it all has a way of
catching up. Bullets ricochet
off any grudge available.

Texas Rangers

Haunting the edge of thought itself,
they pry runaways from the frontier,
freshly nailed shut, sealed
with wax straight from sentry candles,
the only glow left between
white fear and possibility,
the promises we hang on parchment,
use as wadding.

Six lead balls and a hammer,
an eager finger leaves the law
obscured in smoke.

Mustang

Hoof beats wake the scorpions,
send them deeper beneath the stones,
paint the canyon floor with a frenzy
of brawn and high order fear.
I've seen men die in such a picture:
the rapture of motion,
an ocean of sand that leaps toward the sky and
whirlpools in the orange,
the deafening rays of a gloaming star.
Keep all limbs clear of sharp beginnings.
Remember that God's hands will shatter you
before they carry you home.
Lean into the turn, let your knees do the talking,
pull the rope with your whole body, learn
when to let go.

Free Soil Party

The barnburners
astound no one but never shy
from making noise
or being right.

Soak the ground,
let the fuel catch itself and
watch as the roots morph
into ash.

Dead institutions
make way for new tendrils,
green fingers of fresh life,
gonna let liberty grow.

Tecumseh to the Osages

The spirit path springs fire,
runs red, kindles distress.

Shared children,
hungry, sick serpents
invigorate death.

Feeble panthers
ask for our hunting grounds.

Winters made peace,
our mothers cheated the tomahawk,

my tomahawk
will destroy many nations.

Unite the desolate,
rushing waters, angry blood.

Swallow the Mississippi.
Fight for us.

The Railroad Is Coming

Cover your poor ears.
Satan's steam box chews black rock,
sings to high heaven.

Clark's Hill

The things we bury are never as dead as the things we live for. A country of no grandfathers. Too young to heed wise words and with no formative field from which to harvest. We stomp on the heads of kind ghosts. Call it our newly fashioned home. We cross our legs and enjoy the view.

The Boys Come Home

He rolled his bed for the last time,
all but bolted his boots to the floorboards.
Carried a pistol out of habit.
Tilled the dirt with a broken musket.

Stayed up nights, vision-hungry,
paced the bounds of battlefields
to see where he'd gone wrong.
Channels of steady bullets,
crimson rivers that lap at the sky,
flags that never forsake the low ground.

The Abandoned Camp

Maybe the pack slows
when its cubs
start to shed their colors
or when its alphas go gray,
start limping and swaying
under the weight of their earned wisdom.

But that excuse strikes
empty with me.

Maybe, we just try too hard
to ignore the nature of things.
Will ourselves up and over
the needs of the Earth.

Maybe we'll die charting old courses
with new burdens. It seems
the more we know, the more
those burdens begin to weigh.

And maybe at the end of the day,
the wolf and the hunter
are no different, figuring their sharp bite
for the rifle.

But as we walked into that camp,
the old men trembled
like game caught in a steel trap's jaws.
And the little girl
who'd been discarded,
left in a tent to rot
in a puddle of animal thirst,
looked at us
like we had come for our turn.

As if she'd been waiting for us
to end her suffering,
skin her for the fur market
and make feast of her flesh.

Maybe, the wolf and the hunter
are no different, figuring their sharp eyes
for the iron sight.

But I can promise,
you'll never catch me
leaving one of us behind,
or unleashing such beastly evil
on a body so young.

Blood Money

You should hear how they talk of Comanche foot tracks.

You should hear how they cry into the canyon.

You should hear the war stories, gristle still fresh on their canines.

You should hear of pistol grips and antler pipes.

You should hear how many daughters sleep under far away
tree lines, should hear the secret of the crosswinds.

You should hear the secret of berries, how to properly crush, press
    them into red meat,
how the taste of life is one of the few things that make it worth
    fighting for.

You should hear the words they use for money, for bullets, for
whiskey.

You should hear where the scalps come from.

You should ignore your own voice, any impulse to ask any further.

Beecher's Bibles

> "What is written in the scroll pertains to me.
> I want to do what pleases you, my God."
> —Psalm 40:7–8 (NET)

Bible crates packed with Sharps rifles
Marksmen laureled as saints
Halos fetched from Pottawatomie creek
Streams awash with rebirth
Sacred sites where the blood and mud converge
A new body cleansed of death and bondage
Songs of praise etched into barrels
Guns that never stop firing

All the Feathers I Sent Home

Their horse thieves yield fame
Don't even keep the rewards
Slows everyone down

Prairie Thoughts #2

Sherman never knew wind like this

Would have left him as a fameless match

A fizzle at best

A hero knocked onto his back

While the Georgia mosquitos

Strapped on their gray accoutrement

And terrorized each edge of the swamp

Here, all things find their knees in dirt

Bent, a reverent devotion

To unstoppable force

Its shameless reach

Heaven Is a Woman from Tennessee

> "We went into camp for a few days on the outskirts of Memphis . . . The bachelors found an Elysium in the society of many very pretty girls, and love-making went on either in luxurious parlors or in the open air."
> —Elizabeth Bacon Custer, *Boots and Saddles*

Her name was lost
between the drawl and the sounds
of men rearing up for the invasion:
a whole horde of ladies with cups
full of table wine and purses empty
of any and all graces. Not for long.

We love the Southern heat, the sticky air
and its ideas about two bodies
baptized in a river we make ourselves.
She came to me like a vision,
in lace and Turkish blue.
We made love in the grass,
sweating on spread linen,
and I held her, artfully balancing
my cold ego and the warmth
my exiled tears could bring.

A perfect moment suspended
over orders, over crudely shaped words like "Dakota,"
the realization that her Daddy probably lost his life
to a Union musket. For a moment,
tomorrow's thoughts were a generation away,
consequences to be inherited
by some future version of myself.

I was in heaven, somewhere outside Memphis,
whistling to the tune of the breeze.

Six Paces

We all long for spectacle,
the dance of egos in the dust.
A spark that cracks the ears before it burns the nostrils.
At this hour, angry hinges singe the nerves.
Onlookers buy shares in the outcome.

Quick-snap knuckles, oiled leather,
pearl-painted wood
in the palm.

Steady fingers win all dances with death.

Custer at Gettysburg

The saber's sacred law commands
energy forward.

Full-tilt we harrow into blindness,
the rage of ecstasy as it boils our brains
toward deliverance.

The fresh air collides with our eardrums,
hurrying past us, catches on nothing,
ushers us home,
invites his red sash to play in the wind.

Ownership

The sweat in your eye, the sun
tracing every damn second along the back of your neck.
The coals breathe dark sighs of understanding.
Which smells worse, the cowshit
or the brand's kiss? Hold still, hear.
Iron sings into the hide.
This is why
calves are born with a short memory.

Crockett for Congress

Name embroidered
in poorly stitched furs,
the rugged face of the New America.

Fighting over inches, small hovels
stolen, adorned with red paint,
souvenir war clubs.

A shingle hangs on a postless door,
no foundation to keep the frame from sinking.
Here lives your voice.

Big decisions, symbolic apologies
too late and ill-sutured
to mean much of anything.

A Horse Called Dandy

A brute weapon filed down,
softly gnawing the bit of compliance,
slowing to a restful trot.

Heavy holsters, fresh prints,
little receding patches of brown spit.

We will get there when we get there.

Welcome to Yankton

An April blizzard nearly killed us.
It took us out of our beds the first day in camp.
We had to break our backs in the cold.
Tear everything down, wander into town
where it then took our dignity,
left us begging for room and board,
barn, shed, or stable,
anything with a corner
big enough for us to shiver in.
Even this far North, we never saw this coming.
Boys losing fingers, toes. Whole hands and feet
gnawed right off
by the frost's cruel teeth.

The general's still out there
in a commandeered house.
All that rank just to freeze
in a bundle of tired men, hay, and horseshit,
to drag his poor wife to hell's frigid peaks
as wintry gusts of death's breath
lap at their will.

I thought the frontier held a trove
of just endeavors and the rewards
of a life-long job well done.

Surely, I could have found what I'm looking for
in some place that respects the seasons,
where Spring brings green in all its shades
and brings the promise of new life. It brings.
It brings.

It shouldn't take anything from anybody.

Law Rules the Desert Shore

Pick any metal you like. Gilded brooches
carry little more than their market weight.

Thrones bolted behind
desks borrowed from shop clerks.

You're here because we're paying you to be.
Buy your goods local,
keep your pistol loaded.

Don't go to sleep
until the rest of us are snoring.

Prairie Thoughts #3

Heard a private talkin'.
Misses his family's farm
in Ohio. Believe it or not,
they got grass just like this
and treelines brimmin'
with cats and coyotes.
Kept harassing the livestock.
Pa killed so many
'til one day they stopped comin'.

Never did know
if the 'yotes learned their lesson,
or if he killed them all.

One way or the other,
this'll all end.

The Advice of Secretary Delano

"I am a red man. If the Great Spirit had desired me to be a white man he would have made me so in the first place."
—Lakota Tatanka Iyotake (Sitting Bull)

That stone look, in the eyes, so grievous, these somber cartographers keeping their fingers pointed past sunrises, sunsets, cardinal directions on an earthen map picked from their windswept memory, they follow and we follow, this nation of the beef.

We can kill the buffalo and watch as the blood guides us, a navigating heart charts ahead. Nothing brutal about it. We hear their empty stomachs, but this is just what it's like before the new can rise from the wreckage, debris, and dead bodies.

It sounds gruesome, but horns mean war, whether they're shaped in brass or bison gore, we'll get them where it hurts the most, wear their last meal across our backs, taste the viscera in the milkweed and sing

farewell to the prairie folk, farewell to the uncivilized musings of Mother Dirt's better days, her pressure, her storms. We build houses from her limbs, new men from corn whiskey.

We don't need to be scared anymore, never again, we don't need them, but give it a few months. They will need us.

Steer

Snort. Three stomps, the dominant leg. We pray for rain, they beat the dust. And just like that, all is calm again. Doldrum. Mellow patterns in the chaw. An acousmatic gift for anyone who chases composure through the thick of normality, the long green stems of here and now.

Murieta

For men who followed
gold veins into Earth's brittle chest,
chipped away at its core,
its grand cytoplasm of stone and decay,
they sure find their moments
to flounder and rot like beasts.

The thoughtless collapse
of decency.

A pistol glints in the sun.
Light for once,
the warm hand of morning,
an assurance that beginnings
always come at the end of darkness.

Revenge is like freshly cured ham.
It stings the tongue.
Salt and sugar, the way
fat and flesh melt
into sweet sensation.

Justice is like dynamite.
A fuse trimmed too short,
blows up at the wrong time,
hurts the wrong people.

Cacti

What stern words for the sun,
a real tight point of view.
No one likes to be forgotten,
but then again,
blistered skin is a special calling,
and no one can blame a sentinel
for doing its job,
bringing fruit, color to the sand,
forever rejecting comfort,
cool drinks, days that don't require
cloud cover to relax you.

Welcome to Kansas

God is at work here.
Blood becomes a tool sometimes.
Helps the bluestem grow.

Grant Is a Drinkin' Man

His maps and charts diffuse,
takeover each inch of space.

Command is a viral honor.
It infects all time, all sleep, all surfaces.

He sends the others to bed
and pours his sense of daring into a suitable vessel,

a glass that will hold the morning
and its decisive maneuver,

will shape the fog and give direction.
A compass whose needle finds its bearing

when its been drained of its weight-bearing unction,
all traces of magnetic goodwill spilt

before the altar
of a balanced conscience.

A kind of confidence
you have to put on each night.

Custer Never Touches Liquor

> "Look, they are saying, 'Our bones are dry, our hope has perished; we are cut off.' Therefore prophesy, and tell them, 'This is what the Sovereign Lord says: Look, I am about to open your graves and will raise you from your graves.'"
>
> —Ezekiel 37:11–12 (NET)

Work is done with steady hands.
Dry bones water the Earth, even when no one is looking.
A man as tall as his creator.
A hat that never loses form.
Dry bones ask for succor.
Dry roads lead to holiness.
All eyes look up before the battle takes shape.
Some footsteps are more important than others.
Some streets still echo your foolish voice.
Some echoes still haunt your smartest moments.
Strong men never need wasted evenings.
Dry bones ask for tending.
Dry bones want a leader, a man to hang his name in the sky.
Dry bones ask you to bring it down with you.

San Isidro Smiles Over the Western Plains

A buck an acre.
Even small indulgences
buy plots in heaven.

Prairie Thoughts #4

Satchels of eggs cook in the sun.
Guarding flour with gunpowder.

One wonders if supplies
ever get where they're really needed.

If breaking bread makes more sense
than taking it.

Earp

Strategic grooming,
twitched lips and teeth
that can strain tall names through
any crack they choose.

Legends have a way of defending themselves,
spin steel and polish metal as needed,
pose for the womenfolk, remind them
that all ends have merit.

Crazy Horse Scares Us Senseless

A warrior's shirt obscured by low hanging clouds.
The sky here never made sense to me.
It frames the wrong people as heroes.
Casts the hills as playthings.
Lets their cries hover around us
for too damn long.

Marion

"I called this island Bad Humored Island, as we were in a bad humor."
—William Clark

It's important to keep one's eyes open.
Surprise, like all elements of war,
has the grip to take your very soul from you,
leave it stranded and begging for a quick,
sharp reprieve.

I've got resolve, but no desire
to play cards with clever futures,
any name I've ever longed to make for myself.

Economy of force, like all elements of war,
is essential. Worth keeping at all costs.

Tecumseh to Harrison

Land can't wish aloud,
it portents strong boundary,
bad consequences.

Locoweed

We chop the dirt,
grab sickness by the roots. Twist.
Fill our sacks, bruise our necks,
lay it all down at the mounds,
foul piles of purged color,
scooped with sand and blood.
Skin and bones, the kind of hurt
that kills while they're still standing.
It'll all be ash in the morning.

Georgetown

Keep your feet dry, your head down, all threadbare legs away from the sparks. My pick carries more light than the stars, grows heavier with every swing.

When the candle is lit, the silver glitters as you wander into the mouth of the mountain. Waste little, want not. Breathe easy. The Earth is sitting on top of you.

Dry Gulch Saloon

Gaslamp halos,
rumors that sour the glow,
hover, twist names into bad omens.

A corner is no place to live.
Targets named before aim is taken
spill on the creaky floor.

Cattleman's Lullaby

We sang to 'em at night. Let our voices
drip in the dark, steadily stroke
their nerves, keep them down and quiet.
I never saw a place so wide, so full.
And when the stars salted through
the last slices of daylight,
we forgot all about the miles ahead,
the daily pay for sleeping in the dirt.

Pirate Savior of New Orleans

Liberty blossoms in the swamp.

Men who nursed on a curved blade, raised
so their legs could grip the waves, stormed
and emptied the holds of commerce, crafted
names and shared the riches.

They barter, pleasures for comforts
and back again. A long life
built on consensus and scar tissue,
outside the law of proper classes.

A toast for new structures,
trails we clear ourselves,
homes that heave on stilts
over the salty water.

Gentle eyes that navigate the blackness,
starless nights, that always make home
the center, the marsh's flower
from which all compasses can bloom.

David Crockett to Charles Schultz

A short moment
can break Southern hounds loose.

The time of sly power, majority will
to judge the lost, declare elected kingdoms.

I will go to the wildes of Texas,
will consider paradise

as liberty
bows to the yoke of slave owners.

Hope proceeds
on my way home.

San Miguel Chapel

Fervent clay
Confounded frame, statuary
Glimmering child's eye
Aflame and young
Crying to Christ's star
For a blanket of cool air
Gentle fingers to soothe
The face of foundation
Original homes of enrobed men
Brush the mountain pines
Direct the rivers
Bring life into all hills
Quiet prayers, large beads
Settle notions of muscle
Grit teeth, bless
The children
Tie colts in the churchyard
Ride for peace
Back to Jerusalem

Annie Oakley

"There is nothing more dangerous than a woman with a shotgun . . ."
—Louis L'amour

She barked about gentle movement.

Finesse and wonder, rode in wild loops.

Heaven's adulation, crowds tend to mimic thunder.

Golden girl of the sagebrush.

Felt, leather, and silk.

Short speeches on fame's blissful presence.

How opportunity is a moving target.

Why it's important to keep your guns clean.

Prairie Thoughts #5

Our calves swell with adrenaline and clumsy prayers.
We are meat, we are hunted like meat.

Chorus of piebalds,
snorting in the rear distance.

We dive into the creek,
we have faith enough
to carry us to the other side.
Winged heels, we do our best
to skirt the surface,
fly to safety.

Break left or stay to swallow mud.
Live to tell stories about
how your legs will always carry you home
if it really means that much to you.

Red River Gonna Swallow You Whole

I was down and out, and they knew it.
No pennies to drop into the town well,
no wishes to think of.
They promise you a full belly,
too much money for your saddle bag,
and tell stories of big women
in cowtown saloons.
But civilization is lost to me.
All we see are clapboard skylines
that burn their evening fires
while we bed down between the rocks,
pick the charred bits of dinner from our back teeth,
the never-ending gravel of burnt chuck
and uncooked beans.
I never found her. Nothing is beautiful out here.
Even the water comes for you.
It burns the meat of your palm
as you try to wash your wounds,
where your lasso bit you, burned you
for doing your job.
It flows red, it takes you nowhere.

Chief Seattle's Alleged Oration

Compassion may return.

Goodwill can overcast
cruel and relentless forefathers.

Young lives worship love,
forsake the graves of religion.

Sad-voiced descendants
who mourn power, untimely fate.

Great nation, follow the order
of nature. Vanish,

thrill of death.

Pony Express

Flexed brows in the sun,
speedy departures.

Our backs don't break under pressure.

Paper parcels tied with string,
exclamations of subdued ground.

We drill for riches,
but heap success one mouthful at a time,
in distances much shorter than memory.

Weatherford

Surrender is a felled oak.
Swift and heavy,
it drags a corner of the forest
down with it.
The blades have chipped
at its neck long enough.
Gravity, its inevitable brogue,
is a real braggart son of a bitch, some times.

Strong names rot.
The undergrowth, soft
with gradual release, moisture,
animal allies dividing
as is determined by their nature,
will no longer soar
in blood and anger.

Westinghouse

Wind as a brick wall for once.
Iron on iron, we spider crawl
the spines of progress
and release
a stunning sigh of relief.

Migrants Build the West

Wage chains rattle.
Voyages spent groaning, bought
with thanks, a month's work for pocket change.
The bodies still dot the desert.

Turned to rock, absorbing
the blistering rays of our sister star,
shielding tidy traces of sand.

We cover our eyes, glass the horizon.
Sacrifice waves back.
It gives the only gift worth giving,
the kind that can never be repaid.

Saint Francis Ministers to the Owls at Rogue River

Needle-fine pinyon scraps,
a spine, a blue bead.
Some feathers travel
from far oceans,
jungles that rest
in similar rhythms,
chests that rise and beat
along the water's edge.
Where we all once played
and were dealt raw labor,
no beasts of burden
to save our shoulders
from holding up the planet.

Fort Union

Country plum picked
of top-heavy colors.

Just a West that seems to bleed
farther from home by the minute.

The green in the hills is outnumbered.
The sand floats

as streams of mirrored heat
between the trees.

God has abandoned the soil.
But the gray army came anyway,

shooting off the edge of the world
in the name of a nation

that couldn't fit into its own boots.

Custer Dies at Little Bighorn

Men lay in dollops of lifeless color,
like a vegetable garden ransacked
by a strong storm.
Rifles staked as reminders,
the lazily planted seeds of glory.

Dust and blame fall into the cracks,
the gaps between posterity and
everyone's best guesses.

Surely, we haven't forgotten
that battlefields are equalizers.
Life ends and people choose
to honor their intended victors.

Mystery is handed down
in clumsy ceremony, its self-inflicted
scepter of mercy and conjecture.

Meanwhile, our heroes are tossed
to the elements. Left as pin cushions,
ammo pouches,
punchlines, and dirt mounds.

Prairie Thoughts #6

> "Whenever its branch becomes tender and puts out its leaves, you know that summer is near."
>
> —Matthew 24:32 (NET)

A single cottonwood buzzes,
bathed in crooked slats of evening luster.
Perturbed crickets sound reveille
for long dead seasons
of good harvest.

Saplings burn with the old grass.
A lone tree suspended by time
stands watch over the prairie
in pale, rugged defiance.
A rare bastion of life
conquering predictable ends,
any semblance of cycle.

About the Author

Timothy Tarkelly's work has appeared in *Vocivia Magazine, Agape Review, Ekstasis Magazine,* and others. His most recent books include *Polling Data as a Means of Self-expression* (OAC Books) and *Angie and her Roommate* (Alien Buddha Press). When he's not writing, he teaches and coaches debate in Southeast Kansas.

www.ingramcontent.com/pod-product-compliance
Lightning Source LLC
Chambersburg PA
CBHW021328190426
43193CB00039B/489